PRAISE FOR *BUDDHA'S CLOSET*:

"A wise man once said you only lose what you cling to. I couldn't put *Buddha's Closet* down! Color me newly out of the closet and freshly on the path to enlightenment."

CAROLYN MARK, THE BOOZY CHANTEUSE

"Declutter your closet and your thoughts with the profound but simple lessons Kerri lays out for living a mindful life and having a wardrobe that truly reflects you."

KRIS ASHLEY, AUTHOR OF *CHANGE YOUR MIND TO CHANGE YOUR REALITY*

BUDDHA'S CLOSET

CLEANING AS A PATH TO ENLIGHTENMENT

KERRI SCOTT

Kerri Scott Books
VANCOUVER ISLAND, BRITISH COLUMBIA

COPYRIGHT © 2024 BY KERRI SCOTT. All rights reserved. No part of this publication may be reproduced, distributed, or transmitted in any form or by any means, including photocopying, recording, or other electronic or mechanical methods, without the prior written permission of the publisher, except in the case of brief quotations embodied in critical reviews and certain other noncommercial uses permitted by copyright law. For permission requests, contact the author at the website below.

Kerri Scott / Kerri Scott Books
KerriScott.com

Cover design by Gus Yoo
Copy editing and book production by Stephanie Gunning

Special discounts are available to librarians and on quantity purchases by corporations, associations, and others. For details, contact the publisher.

Buddha's Closet / Kerri Scott —1st edition
ISBN 978-1-7383961-0-8 (paperback)
ISBN 978-1-7383961-1-5 (ebook)

Dedicated to you.

The unchanging Self in me recognizes the unchanging Self in you.

CONTENTS

PREFACE	xi
CHAPTER 1. The Eight-Fold Path	1
CHAPTER 2. Slow Style	9
CHAPTER 3. Tickled Pink	17
CHAPTER 4. Mind Full, or Mindful?	25
CHAPTER 5. Say "Yes!"	29
CHAPTER 6. Retail Therapy	41
CHAPTER 7. Maya	51
CHAPTER 8. Sole Searching	59
CHAPTER 9. Sadhana	71
ACKNOWLEDGMENTS	79
CITATIONS	81
RESOURCES	83
ABOUT THE AUTHOR	84

PREFACE

How did I go from resenting housework and cleaning to finding it a fulfilling spiritual practice?

I haven't always been a perimenopausal mom with hot flashes in her late forties. In fact, there was a time when I was behind at the hormone game, a late bloomer, as they say. It was the Nineties, so naturally I wore thrifted flannel plaid shirts, Grandpa Pants (as we called them back then), loads of corduroy (also the name of my favorite martini), wide-legged pants, waffle-top shirts, and Simple skate shoes.

My wardrobe wasn't all khaki green and brown. There was some dusty rose in it, too. Over the decades, clothing styles have come and gone. Today, although I still love muted, natural tones, I have expanded the range of colors and fabrics I dare to wear. These include bright primary colors and sequins and metallics, but pink corduroy stands out as one of my favorites.

If you are anything like me, a fashionista, and you love everything to do with clothing, style, and fashion, it's possible that your friends and family will call you vain or narcissistic because, like me, you can't pass a mirror without looking at yourself. My high school sweetheart called me out for what he believed was self-obsessed behavior. He would shake his head at me in the mall when I did a second take in the mirrors we passed. I didn't understand his frustration. I was genuinely curious about the person I saw in my reflection.

I held no clear mental image of who I was—but I wanted one. Even as a teenager, I was seeking something, some sort of spark of self-awareness that I believed recognizing my own reflection might hold. Behavior that appeared from outside me to be vanity really was rooted in my deep longing to know myself.

In this book, *Buddha's Closet*, I will show you that exploring the passion we feel for self-expression through our clothing and adornments can be an important part of a deeper exploration of our true Self. I say, take all the clothes out of the closet and look at them in the light.

So, who am I to write a spiritual guidebook on cleaning out your closet? Well, that ultimately is the question we all must ask as we embark on our spiritual awakening. *Who am I?*

Returning to the Nineties for a moment, my first glimpse of my spirituality came at a weeklong hatha yoga class at Naramata Centre, a retreat and conference center in the Okanagan Valley of British Columbia in Canada. If I could compare the experience of that weeklong workshop to trying on clothes, it was like taking off my prom dress and putting on pajamas. Sweet comfort! I loved the movement and the philosophy. Yoga wasn't just postures; it was an entire way of living.

Before learning about yoga, I was trying to fit into spiritual beliefs that often felt uncomfortable, as though they didn't belong to me. Yoga was an invitation to look at myself differently. It welcomed me inwards, to explore my breath and energy while challenging me both mentally and physically. This was my first experience with awareness, and it felt incredibly illuminating, as though I was finally able to recognize myself in the reflection of the mirror.

These teachings intrigued me and, while I did my undergraduate degree in astrophysics, I also took classes in yoga and eastern religion. Academically, I pursued science, but my heart was always in fashion and design. In the summers, I ventured off to New York to study fashion design at Parsons School of Design and to Vancouver to work as a seamstress in a boutique clothing store. After graduation, my career path flip-flopped between science and fashion, until I put on my mom jeans in 2011.

As a stay-at-home mom, when my husband was at his job and the kids were in school, I used to spend my alone time sewing and blogging. Then, on my fortieth birthday, I had a spiritual awakening. I like to say three things had to happen for my awakening to begin. First, I had to believe that everything is energy, which I learned in my studies in physics. Second, I had to take full responsibility for my life, no more blaming others or feeling like a victim. Third, I had to experience grief after losing someone I deeply cared for.

As I began a journey of personal growth, inspired by the breathwork I learned in my first yoga class, blogging turned into researching and writing about the spiritual lessons that were unfolding for me. Conflicted because I was no longer earning an income, I studied and wrote, feeling stressed and compelled to prove my worth by keeping my family's home clean. The trouble was, I resented doing housework and struggled to make it routine. It quickly became clear that even if I cleaned all the time, our house would be, at best, tidy. I still felt like a victim to cleanliness.

While each time I hauled another Rubbermaid tote in or out of our three-foot-tall crawlspace under our house with the door located outside, beneath my bedroom window, I was overwhelmed by the fact that my life had boiled down to managing stuff. Yet, any time I organized a space, be it a single drawer or the entire garage, there was a simultaneous shift in energy in another aspect of my life. By clearing stuck and stagnant energy in one place, I apparently was inviting new and exciting ideas and inspiration into other areas of my life. Just like the emotional energy work I was learning about, by physically clearing spaces in my home, I was inviting new energy to flow through. This phenomenon interested me.

Now I call myself a *householder*, a not-so-common name for many of us who are following the spiritual seeker's path while living life in society. Cleaning is my guru, or spiritual teacher. Householders such as me work, play, love, and have families, which differs from the path of a devoted monk who retreats from ordinary relationships. Hopefully, we can still carve out time to practice meditation and gratitude or some delightful combination of meaningful modalities in between managing our other obligations.

Cleaning can be a meditation, like any other, and just like with more conventional meditation, we may have initial reluctance to doing it. The first step is wanting to clean. (Much of the time, we do not have the desire.) Householders may not worship in a temple, but our homes are sacred spaces where we can contemplate the nature of Self and practice self-inquiry.

Unlike a monk, householders own stuff. Some of us have houses, cars, furniture, patio furniture, dishes, and cutlery. These objects, often useful or unused, fill the spaces we occupy, and oftentimes—just like everybody else's—our closets and dressers are brimming with clothing, shoes, and accessories.

Just as often as I trip over shoes at my front door, I am stumbling along my spiritual path, trying on many spiritual modalities. I learned reiki and investigated *The Gene Keys*. Tapping, tarot, Human Design, kundalini yoga, attending satsang meditations, and breathwork have all been styles of spiritual expression that I have worn. Some have passed through my life like trends; others have become timeless classic forms of *sadhana*, or spiritual exercise, for me.

One of the most potent reoccurring messages I have received from Spirit as I journey along my path is to be playful. And where would I have the most fun but in my closet? When I spend an hour or so trying on clothes, organizing my belongings, and creating a seasonal wardrobe, I feel an immense amount of joy. There is a movement of energy that occurs whenever I take the time to pull all my clothing out of the closet, pile it on the bed, and experiment with new color combinations, textures, sounds, and even smells. I thoroughly enjoy rediscovering clothes that I have not worn in quite some time.

Each time I play in my closet and allow it to be an act of self-love and spiritual inquiry, I get to solve the deeper mystery of who I am. The joy of changing my clothes helps me reflect that I am unchanging—or, as my satsang teacher, Hirdaya, says, "You are unchanging, forever free, and pure."

The ritual of cleaning out our closets with the seasons may be the closest many of us will get to becoming monks, but my hope is to share with you three things I have learned in my closet:

1. Everything is your guru.
2. Be playful on the spiritual path.
3. Practice self-love by knowing who you are at the core: You are unchanging.

There are so many words to describe what it is that we seekers are looking for on our spiritual path. It is a state of being. The name of this state differs from tradition to tradition, from psychology to physiology, and from teacher to teacher. Some of its names include the true Self or true nature, *atman*, *satya*, or *samadhi*, peak experience, or Buddha nature. It can also be called awareness or consciousness, which are designations that I find get confusing. For the sake of simplicity, I will refer to this state as the recognition and embodiment of your unchanging Self.

My inner child loves to play in my closet so that is also what this book is about. I will be walking you through a step-by-step process to clean out your closet and create an inspired seasonal wardrobe. But ultimately it is about finding your own joy and recognizing it within you when it arises.

ONE

THE EIGHT-FOLD PATH

"You need to learn how to select your thoughts just the same way you select your clothes every day." [1]

ELIZABETH GILBERT

Before we pull up our sleeves and get to work in our closets, let's talk a little more about this state of being, the unchanging Self, which I referred to in the Preface. Sometimes it easier to explain something by telling what it is *not* rather than what it is. So, I will do that now.

I think most of us can agree that we spend a lot of our lives longing to feel better. We often have thoughts like *I will be happy when (fill in the blank)*. To feel better, we might seek approval from others, most often our loved ones, or authority figures. For instance, we might work hard to attain a title, attending a school to get a certificate or degree, to prove our worthiness to our parents or colleagues.

We might also do things, such as eating certain foods (my favorite is chocolate), to get a feeling of satisfaction. But for some reason, this sense of satisfaction that we gain never seems to last. I always want more chocolate even after I eat chocolate.

Another desire always comes to replace the first one once it is fulfilled. This is clear when we look at the belongings in our closets. We go shopping to find fulfillment in an item that we buy. But once that item comes home with us, it doesn't take long for us to lose the sense of fulfillment we first felt when we bought it, and then another new desire for something else takes its place.

This is human nature. We have what seems like an insatiable desire for fulfillment, and we believe that something external, be it clothing, food, achievements, or a person can give it to us. The irony of amassing possessions is that once we have collected many things, we believe we will feel better once we declutter. Recognizing this as a pattern that we take part in, we can begin to observe when these desires arise in us and witness how we respond when they are fulfilled or not fulfilled. This state as the recognition and embodiment of your unchanging Self is that of finding fulfillment without the need for external validation.

True fulfillment is a state of well-being and satisfaction that arises from within. It is not a place that you arrive at, but rather it is a knowing that you return to. It is your most natural state of being and you will recognize it by how good it feels when you find it within yourself. This is what I mean when I say that this book is ultimately about finding your own joy and recognizing it within you when it arises.

BUDDHA'S CLOSET

To begin, I would like to introduce you to my eight-fold process of closet cleaning. I say this with tongue in cheek because it's highly likely we won't be folding anything, and because the Buddha's Noble Eightfold Path doesn't talk about clothing anywhere as far as I know. Yet the two paths do have one thing in common: Both emphasize the importance of bringing your awareness to your thoughts.

Along my spiritual journey I've noticed many spiritual concepts being shared as fashion metaphors. The first one that I encountered was this idea of "cute little matching baggage." International business consultant Monique Alvarez shared this concept in an online business workshop I attended, and I immediately fell in love with it. I have a cute set of matching pink plaid luggage that I store in my closet between vacations. They stand out and are so easy to recognize at the baggage claim carousel in any airport.

But the metaphor that Monique was referring to in relation to personal growth was that we all have our own limiting beliefs, hence her use of the term *baggage*. Limiting beliefs are often one of the first concepts we learn when we begin to bring our awareness to our thoughts. These are thought patterns that we may not know that we have that hold us back in some way. They limit our behavior and can keep us from achieving a goal or stepping out of our comfort zone.

Self-sabotaging thoughts, low self-esteem, perfectionism, self-criticism, imposter syndrome, or a scarcity mindset, to name just a few factors, can cause you to dim your light rather than becoming extra visible, like plaid luggage.

Unresolved traumas can create fears: fear of failure, fear of rejection, fear of intimacy, and fear of success. By bringing your awareness to these limiting aspects of your belief system, you can begin to overcome these self-imposed limitations.

Sometimes when we read about a limiting belief it illuminates it within us. You may not be aware that a certain belief influences your behavior because you identify with it so strongly. I have posted a list of common limiting beliefs that may help you uncover your limiting beliefs. You can download it on my website, KerriScott.com.

I collect fashion metaphors that can be applied to personal and spiritual growth because of my passion for both spirituality and fashion. As I mentioned in the Preface, Spirit often reminds me to be playful on my spiritual journey, and one of the places that play comes naturally to me is in my closet. It is a space where my inner child can be seen, and I give her full permission to be creative and explore all my clothing and accessories.

What I discovered through playful exploration is that my closet is a metaphor for my mind and my clothes are a metaphor for my thoughts. Therefore, each step of my eight-fold process is also a metaphor for spiritual growth. Just as we choose the clothes that we wear each day, we ought to choose the thoughts that we think. Or thoughts should not be choosing *us*—meaning, how we define ourselves and behave.

With intention, the clothes we put into our seasonal wardrobe will be handpicked by us just like the thoughts we choose to think.

If you have ever woken up at two in the morning and can't fall back asleep because you are worried about something you said to someone the day before or a task that you are required to do at work the next day, then you know how persistent thoughts can be. It is human to try to distract ourselves from our thoughts when they seem too painful or difficult to acknowledge. But what if there were a way to handle those troubling thoughts without ignoring them? An emotionally healthier option?

Any time you are still, your thoughts seemingly take over your mind. Intentionally bringing your awareness to your thoughts during stillness and letting them go is a form of meditation. This is better for our well-being than repression.

There are many forms of meditation we can do. Any time we are engaged in an activity that allows our thoughts to rise so we can witness them and let them pass is a form of mindfulness. Yoga, walking, art, and even cleaning can all be considered forms of meditation because we are allowing ourselves to be present with our thoughts when we do them.

In *A Monk's Guide to a Clean House and Mind*, Shin-Buddhist monk Shoukei Matsumota writes: "We sweep dust to remove our worldly desires. We scrub dirt to free ourselves of attachments. The time we spend carefully cleaning out every nook and cranny of the temple grounds is extremely fulfilling. We live simply and take time to contemplate the self, mindfully living each moment. It's not just monks who need to live this way."[2] I agree with him wholeheartedly.

So, as you clean out your closet, do your best to be present with the thoughts that each item of clothing represents and allow cleaning to become a mindful practice.

My eight-fold cleaning process will require you to bring your attention to all the clothing in your closet one item at a time in a manner that reveals your thoughts and feelings. If each item stands for a specific thought and your closet is a metaphor for your mind, you may discover, for example, that you have "hanger management" issues. Whether you are currently angry or just chronically messy, by doing the work of bringing your attention to each item of clothing one by one, you are practicing awareness. Awareness is the key to spiritual growth.

Now this is not your typical guide to cleaning out your closet, as you may have guessed. Traditionally, the advice for cleaning out your closet tells you to remove each item from its shelf or hanger, and decide right then and there which pile you are going to place it in. Is it a "keep," a "maybe," or a hard "no, it has to go."

The process that I am introducing you to in this book differs in three ways. First, you don't make any decisions about what stays or goes until much later in the process.

Second, there is a connection with your unchanging Self that I lead you to discover before you make any of these decisions. This is the state of well-being mentioned above.

Third, this whole process should be enjoyable. So often I hear people sharing how cleaning out their closet is a huge, daunting task, and anything but fun. But like Spirit says, I am encouraging you to be playful while you clean out your closet.

You are not here because I am a house-cleaning guru like Marie Kondo or a feng shui-decluttering expert Denise Linn; rather, you are here because you desire an experience of your closet as your guru. Your clothes as your guru.

Maybe you have tried many different methods of cleaning out your closet and purging your wardrobe because you have been told that you need to declutter to be fulfilled. Or you have tried to create the perfect capsule wardrobe to ease your mind and reduce decision fatigue. I have done all these closet cleanouts too, and what I notice, time and time again, is that I am trying to meet someone else's version of what is acceptable. If my closet is organized, then I will feel "good enough." Or if I declutter my possessions, then I will "be successful."

These methods promise fulfillment that is temporary. But my hope is for you to discover fulfillment that is ever lasting. By sharing my eight-fold process with you, I can show you how fulfillment can arise within you by playing in your closet and then you will be able to apply it in all aspects of your life.

These eight steps I advocate are Clarify, Clear, Clean, Change, Celebrate, Create, Contemplate, and Conclude. I have intentionally chosen words beginning with the letter C because I love alliteration almost as much as I adore monochromatic outfits. This is my own personal process that I am sharing with you from which you can take what works for you and leave what doesn't.

Of course, I will go into detail to describe each step of the process in the following chapters. Meanwhile, here is a brief explanation of the journey ahead of you.

- *Step 1.* Here we **Clarify** what values we have about the clothing we own as well as clarifying what intention is leading us to clean out our closet right now.
- *Step 2.* **Clear,** this is where we roll up our sleeves and take everything out of the closet. We move those items into an open space where we can see everything we have collected.
- *Step 3.* **Clean** is when we dust the empty shelves, rearrange our empty hangers, and sweep the floor of the closet before we put anything back into it.

- *Step 4.* **Change** is "wear" we get to change multiple times, putting our best foot forward while doing some "sole" searching. (Both puns intended.)
- *Step 5.* **Celebrate** is why we are here! We are discovering who we truly are, unchanging. (After you celebrate, you may never look at yourself or your closet the same way!)
- *Step 6.* **Create.** We determine some helpful words to guide the outfits we create to hang back up in our seasonal wardrobe.
- *Step 7.* **Contemplate.** Here we examine the relationship between our clothing and thoughts. For instance, we ask what memories are associated with each item of clothing.
- *Step 8.* **Conclude.** We address all the items remaining and answer questions like: Do I need it for work (or another activity)? Does this have a hole in it? Can I consign it or donate it?

Intrigued? Then let's get started.

TWO

SLOW STYLE

"Why do Buddhists meditate in front of mirrors?
For self-reflection!" ³

BEANO JOKES TEAM

As you take this first preparatory step, hopefully you agree that you are here because you are looking for a more playful and satisfying experience cleaning out your closet. Let's get curious and clarify what types of thoughts, beliefs, habits, and values you bring to your clothing choices.

STEP 1: CLARIFY

I have reached a place in my life—*midlife* as it is often referred to—where I have acquired a great many things. My kitchen is full of all the necessary utensils and appliances. My bookshelves are packed with books, and as I mentioned earlier, my crawlspace has many storage totes of toys, craft supplies, camping gear, holiday decorations, and clothes. I love clothes, and I have many of them.

From a young age, I have been obsessed with fashion. To me fashion is an industry and an art that inspires individual style. Fashion changes with the seasons and creates trends, while personal style is how we take what is presented in fashion and make it our own. My clothing is an expression of who I am, and the values that I hold as an individual. Values like comfort, environmental awareness, visibility, sustainability, and spirituality. Curious to find a way for my style to embody my spirituality, it wasn't until I embraced playing in my closet that I made the connection between clothing and spirituality.

It is important to take some time to clarify what values you have about the clothing that you own as well as to clarify your intention for cleaning out your closet.

Think about the stage of life you are in and where you spend your time. Consider your shopping habits, as well as your laundry habits. For instance, I have very few items of clothing that require dry cleaning as that is something that does not fit into my lifestyle. I much prefer to be able to machine wash and dry most of my clothes.

HOT UNDER THE COLLAR

I personally struggle with the vast amount of waste that the fashion industry creates. On numerous occasions, I have asked myself, *How can I participate in an industry that causes so much harm? How can I continue to buy clothes and pass them on without considering the global impact of my actions?* It is overwhelming to understand the destruction that clothing production has caused, from the use of chemical dyes that pollute water sources, to the piles of textile waste that go into landfill, and the human cost of labor and unsafe working conditions.

Over the years, I have experimented with ways to be part of the solution rather that part of the problem. I have designed new clothing using vintage clothes. I did a year-long zero-waste design project where I designed and produced a garment each week for one year that used only, and entirely, one yard of fabric. Also, I have supported local designers and designers that use hemp fabric (a particular passion of mine). And I am an avid thrift store shopper. I take my children's gently used clothing and mine to consignment stores or donate them.

But in this exploration, what I discovered is that the most sustainable items of clothing are the ones that already exist which we wear the most. For example, the underwear that we wear daily is more sustainable than a wedding dress that, for most of us, will only be worn once. The more use we get out of an item of clothing before it becomes landfill, the better.

Understanding this, during my closet cleanouts, I shop the clothes that I already own first, and I rarely get rid of anything, unless it meets a strict list of criteria. (I will discuss these in chapter nine.)

In my home, I have the luxury of storage space, but you may not have as much storage as me, or this approach to "shopping" may not appeal to your values or your living situation. Still, I encourage you to experiment with it and experience the benefits.

This approach is a practice in loving what I have as much as it is about cleaning. Rather than seeking out something new to find gratification, I must first do my best to love the clothes I already own by finding new and exciting ways to wear them.

Some questions you can ask yourself to help gain clarity are:
- Is decluttering my closet my priority?
- Are comfort and fit important to me?
- Is there a certain item of clothing I would like to wear more often?
- Is sustainability important to me?
- Is there a certain business or organization that I would like to support when I consign or donate used clothing?
- Do I consider myself a minimalist or a maximalist?
- Am I following a trend for the season or am I building a timeless and classic wardrobe?

This is a good time for me to clarify the difference between my use of the words *closet* and *wardrobe*. When I refer to *closet*, I am speaking about the physical space that holds your clothes and other items you store in it. It may be a walk-in closet or a pass-though closet. It could be a clothing rack that is not enclosed. It could also be a dresser where you store clothing or a combination of all of these.

Now, when I refer to *wardrobe*, I mean the selection of clothing that you have chosen to put in your closet at any given time. Wardrobe can also mean the physical structure that you store clothing in, but that is not how I am using this term in this book.

This is also a good time to clarify what I mean by the term *seasonal wardrobe*. Seasons in fashion are typically spring, summer, fall, and winter—matching the weather. According to Shin-Buddhist monk Shoukei Matsumota, at his monastery they change their wardrobe or outfits (as they only have two different types of robes) in the spring and autumn.[4]

But a seasonal wardrobe could also be created when there is a new season in your life. You could be transitioning from work to home or home back to the office. A season could simply mean that you bought a new item of clothing, and you are excited to devise new outfits that incorporate it. Or maybe you have a new hairstyle that you are keen to match with your clothing.

Although it makes sense to follow the physical changing of the seasons in transitioning our wardrobes, there are many seasons in our lives, so don't feel limited as to when to play in your closet.

KID GLOVES

As I mentioned before, I have tried restricting myself to a capsule wardrobe. A couple years ago I decluttered my closet and created a monochromatic wardrobe that was composed primarily of white clothing. (This was when I was learning about Kundalini yoga.) It was like a palate cleanse between courses in a restaurant. I have also made twenty outfits and hung each one in its entirety on a single hanger. I could simply grab an outfit and get dressed without much consideration.

Where I have landed after various attempts to control my closet, is that my wardrobe is an ever-changing reflection of my values. I appreciate having a variety of selection at any given time in my wardrobe, but I do not enjoy having all my clothing in my closet. I love rediscovering pieces that have been out of sight and out of mind, so to speak.

And I like each seasonal wardrobe to have an overarching theme or sense of unification. This is where my value of visibility comes into play. The articles of clothing that I am drawn to and wish to wear more often are the items with the boldest colors, prints, and textures. I enjoy getting noticed when I am out and about, and complimented for my outfit. This happens most often when I am wearing a bright color or something with an eye-catching detail.

All my values come together into what I term *slow style*. It's kinda like the term *slow fashion*, but it is the curation of my wardrobe, slowly, over time. I have had to give myself grace when it comes to sustainability, because I can't be perfect at it. I have chosen the best ways that work for me and my lifestyle, which include shopping from what I already own and thrift-store shopping. I will continue to try to improve my environmental footprint. I also enjoy adding items of clothing to my wardrobe, and I am tickled pink when I find a beautiful locally made item of clothing, made from natural fibers that fits in my budget. These items literally check all the boxes for me.

Metaphorically speaking, when it comes to my mind, I also can clarify what intentions to set as I bring my awareness to all my thoughts.

This first step is a bit like stepping back and looking at our mind from a wider perspective. We know we have a mind, and we know we think thoughts, but how much do we identify with these thoughts?

For most of my life, I was simply reacting to the thoughts that I had. I didn't know that I could control the thoughts I was thinking; instead, it felt like my thoughts were in control of me. I was completely identified with my thoughts. If I had an anxious thought, I *was* anxious. If I had a fearful thought, I *was* fearful. If I had a pleasant thought, I *was* happy. As I awakened, I learned that I could separate myself from my thoughts.

This is where meditation becomes so valuable as a personal-growth practice. I learned how to watch my thoughts come into my mind and then let them go, rather than hold on to them and react to them. I curated my thoughts. So, just as we are clarifying the values we have about our clothing and the intentions we have for our closet, we might be curious about the quality of our thoughts and which beliefs form our identity.

Now, let's roll up our sleeves and get messy!

THREE

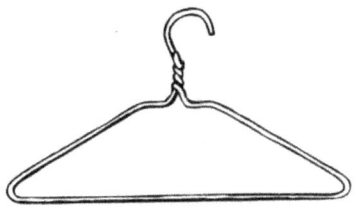

TICKLED PINK

Sometimes we need to get lost to find ourselves.

Our goal with the eight-fold path of closet cleaning is to take all our clothes out of our closet, then edit them, so we keep only the ones that inspire us and feel great wearing, but first we need a place to put them.

STEP 2: CLEAR

Depending on how many clothes you have, the space where you choose to collect everything may differ. I prefer to use my bed as my collection station because it is right next to my closet, and it is a wonderfully spacious, and relatively flat surface to work on. I admit, I rarely make my bed from day to day, but for this occasion, I love to straighten the pillows and pull the comforter up tight to neatly wrap the mattress like a clean, white canvas.

Of course, you could also use the floor, if it's clean, or whatever surface space is available to you.

I recommend setting aside a couple of hours to go through this process, but you might like to stretch it out over a day or two. Therefore, your bed might not be the best staging area, as sleep is particularly important.

There are a few other items you should gather at this time that you will be using during this entire playful process of discovery and editing.

- A mirror
- A dust cloth, broom, and vacuum
- Music (optional): Put it on and get ready to shake your booty
- Your camera (optional)
- A journal (optional)

The most important item is a mirror, preferably a full-length mirror. I have one in my walk-in closet. If you don't have one in the room you plan to use to assess your clothing, then go grab one from another part of your home and bring it close. If you can avoid strutting yourself past your roommate, your partner, husband and kids, or anyone else at home, you will be so much more committed to the results.

I suppose you could also use your phone camera like a mirror to look at yourself in the outfits you will be trying on, but the bigger the mirror the better. I don't care what your hair looks like, if your teeth are brushed, what underwear you are wearing, if you are wearing any makeup, or what your makeup looks like. I only care that you are enthusiastic about playing in your closet and trying on a bunch of clothes!

You are literally going to take everything out of your closet and bring it into the light. Metaphorically, we are illuminating our thoughts. We are warming up the part of ourselves that is the observer, or the witness, of all that we think, believe, and feel.

DON'T AIR YOUR DIRTY LAUNDRY!

Just as we are jumping in, this is an interesting time to examine your closet. What do you typically wear? What is in your laundry basket? Laundry is so telling for me, because the clothes that I wear are only a fraction of the clothes that I own. I would say that I wear about 1 percent of my wardrobe, and of that, 50 percent are fuzzy pajamas. Likely 15 percent are work-specific clothes, 10 percent are clothes that I wear outside of my home, and the remaining 25 percent are socks and underwear. It is quite shocking to me when I "do the math," so to speak.

Keep in mind, I am a perimenopausal stay-at-home mom who spends her days writing and does commercial cleaning on the occasional evening and every other weekend. But it is still shocking! And like our minds, the thoughts that we think tend to be the same few that we keep thinking. These repetitive thoughts then become our beliefs.

So, if I can change my clothes, can I change my thoughts? I believe that, *yes*, we all can.

Okay, with this idea of change in mind, it is time to take all our clothes and pile them on a flat surface. If you are in your bedroom, this will likely be your bed. Any clothes that are in the laundry basket should be washed. You will work these back into your wardrobe once they are clean.

This step, Clear, may seem a bit daunting, particularly if you own a lot of clothes. You could begin to feel lost under the pile of clothing you are creating with items drawn from the recesses of your closet. But don't panic, sometimes we need to get lost to find ourselves.

Working item by item, take each piece of clothing off its hanger, off its shelf, out of its drawer, and out of the closet. Place it in a pile with similar garments. For instance, create a pile of short-sleeved tee-shirts, another for long-sleeved tee-shirts or blouses, and ones for tank tops, pants, shorts, blazers, sweaters, PJs, and so forth. Form whatever types of piles make sense for the clothing items you have in your personal wardrobe.

FINE-TOOTHED COMB

Go slowly and take time to notice which items surprise you as you rediscover them in your collection and move them to the appropriate pile. Make a mental note of which pieces you are longing to wear more often. Maybe there's a fantastic coat you hardly ever wear. Or is there a color that you wish to wear more often but feel intimidated by? Perhaps you possess a silky tank top that is waiting for a special occasion.

Don't do anything with this information yet except notice. Awareness is all you are after as you clear out the closet.

Some items in your closet might feel so special that you hesitate to take them off their hangers for fear of spoiling them. Notice these feelings and impressions too, then take then off the hangers and put them in the pile. Everything must come out.

BUDDHA'S CLOSET

Observe if any clothes still have the store tags on them. Interesting? Pay mind to the colors, textures, prints, and patterns, sounds of the fabric rustling, and even smells as the clothing emerges from its resting place. You are meant to touch each item as it leaves your wardrobe and allow it to invoke a sensation in you.

It wasn't long ago that I bought a pair of hot pink corduroy pants. The joy of finding them still bubbles up inside of me when I take them out of my closet. It was an instant knowing that these pants were destined to me mine. Time stood still, like in a romantic comedy, when two lovers meet for the first time. Classical music started playing in my mind and the voices of my children became silent as I moved toward them in the store. Those pants embodied me in every sense of the word. They were wide-legged, wide-ribbed corduroy, hot pink, and cuddled up on a rack in the store with a few pairs of beige pants when they came to my attention. I found what I thought was my size and bought them without trying them on.

On the way home from the store, while my husband drove the car, I texted three of my girlfriends about the pink pants, and instantly they understood why I was so excited. Unfortunately, when I got home and tried them on, they didn't fit well. My disappointment was raw. The cut was high-waisted, so even though I could zip them up, there was no way I could ever sit down in them. I seriously considered standing for the rest of my life but decided that keeping them wasn't an option. What was an option was searching for a bigger pair.

Long story short, I returned to the store and while waiting in line to return them, I ordered the very last pair, which was my size, online. I would have ordered two pair if I could have!

It is very possible that each item of clothing which comes out of your closet has an origin story of its own. You might notice certain memories arising with certain items of clothes. Pants like mine that you were tickled pink to buy, or others that you regret buying. Certain items might make you feel bad that you haven't worn them, whereas others might remind you of certain people.

Try not to get caught up in any one thought for too long. Simply notice it and allow it to pass. We will discuss these types of thoughts more in chapter eight.

In addition to emptying your closet, be sure to go through your dresser and take out all your socks, swimwear, and scarves, and pile those on your bed too. You can do this with your underwear as well, but simply set them aside. There's a different process for intimates, which I'll discuss with you in chapter eight.

Put your shoes in a pile on the floor.

TIGHTEN YOUR BELT

At this point, all that may be left in your closet are stray items, like purses and accessories. In my dresser, I have a drawer of belts that I share with my husband (the drawer, not usually the belts) and a drawer full of jewelry. If you've got stuff like that hanging somewhere in your closet or dresser, take it out and put it in a neat pile where it won't get damaged.

As I mentioned in chapter one, I keep our matching luggage set in the closet, tucked away under my husband's hanging clothes. There are also a few random items that have been hidden away in my closet, like a set of oil paints that I don't want any one in my house to use, just yet . . . and Ted, my favorite 1980's vintage white Hudson Bay teddy bear. He was supposed to be a birthday present for my best friend in kindergarten, except I loved him so much I wanted to keep him. I threw the biggest temper tantrum of my life (aside from the tequila-invoked temper tantrum I had once at a wedding with my not-yet-husband. Thank goodness for his patience!) Angrily crying, I dramatically demanded to retain ownership of Ted. My five-year-old self was rewarded for my passionate display of desire and Ted became mine.

My point: Don't think too much about these extraneous items but get them out of the closet in the interim and tuck them off to the side somewhere so you can clean.

Also, check the other closets in your home for items of clothing. Do you keep clothes in a second or guest bedroom? Maybe there are a few sweaters by the front door, a scarf on a hook in the front hall closet, a few items for mending in a sewing room. Check your laundry area and be sure to collect any clothes that might have been hung out to dry. (Assuming they are already dry.) Be diligent with yourself and put it all in a heap on the bed. One of these might be the *piece de résistance* that an outfit needs to make it outstanding.

I keep seasonal clothes for summer and winter in plastic totes in a crawl space beneath the first floor of our house, so I am hauling these bins out and sorting through their contents as well.

As you are clearing, collecting, and sorting each item of clothing into piles, you can also begin to organize your thoughts. Author and mindset coach Kris Ashley suggests sorting your thoughts into three categories: "your wants, your fears, and where you're unfulfilled."[5] I love this idea of heaping your thoughts into three distinct piles.

If this feels too complicated, I recommend simply naming the associated feeling that comes with a thought and noticing if your thought is about the past, present or future. Does this thought make you happy or sad? Angry or elated? Do you feel worried about the future or anxious about the past?

When I began to pay attention to my thoughts, I realized how many different types of thoughts there are. Memories, daydreams, fears, limiting beliefs, ideas, worries, judgments, comparisons, and opinions; and then there are plans, goals, and hopes. Our thoughts can then be described as creative, rational, logical, skeptical, discursive, or idle, just to name a few.

So, there is no shortage of piles you can create to sort each thought into as you bring your awareness to them.

Once you've cleared your closet and collected your clothing items in one place, it is time to move on to step three! Clean.

FOUR

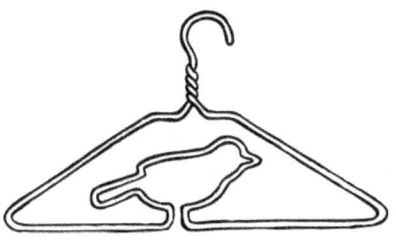

MIND FULL, OR MINDFUL?

Why was the closet always a mess?
It was tired of keeping things neatly tucked away.

At this point everything should be out of your closet, except for hangers and maybe some of those cute lavender sachets or cedar moth balls (I have these in my closet drawers, which is why I mention them.)

Now, it is time to clean.

STEP 3: CLEAN

Dust all the shelves in your closet with a dust rag or duster. Give each drawer a thorough wipe out. Sweep or vacuum the floor and shake out the rug if you have one. Clean the cobwebs out of the corners. And, as appropriate, clean any light fixtures, mirrors, or windows.

I like to geek out and organize my hangers according to type, doing literal hanger management. (This makes it simpler to put them back later.) I group all the white plastic ones together, all the fuzzy nonslip ones together, and all the wide, wooden ones in another group. Then there are the clear plastic hangers that come from stores. I don't usually keep these, but they can be great to have if they are pants hangers. I never seem to have enough of those. These are my personal preferences.

After you have cleaned the shelves and wiped out the drawers, don't forget to wipe down each of the hanging bars too. It is probably time to put your first load of wet laundry in the dryer.

As an aside, I must tell you about the most glorious feather duster I came across while I was Christmas shopping. It looked like the one in Disney's *Beauty and the Beast*, mind you a little less animated. But when I held it in my hand, it made the act of dusting feel elevated, even glamorous. It is no Swiffer Duster. But it feels like the *crème da la crème* of cleaning implements and I can't seem to stop thinking about it. (Maybe dusting with it will be my reward for finishing writing this chapter!)

Don't overlook the importance of this step. Cleaning your now-empty closet creates a sacred space for you to return your clothes to. And if your closet is a metaphor for your mind, when you start with a clear head, you can begin the process of deciding exactly what thoughts you want to fill your mind in the future.

I really enjoy this moment of cleaning out my closet. A sense of calm comes over me when my closet is clean and empty. This emptiness is like the space between my thoughts in meditation.

BUDDHA'S CLOSET

The more I practice meditation, the more attuned I have become to this pause, sometimes it is referred to as a *pregnant void* or *pure presence,* where everything and nothing coexist.

Take a moment to pause and appreciate your clean closet. Feel free to post a photo of your empty space on your social pages and tag #buddhascloset when you do.

FIVE

SAY "YES!"

Change is the only constant.

Now you will begin to invent outfits using all the clothes you have pulled out of your closets and drawers.

STEP 4: CHANGE

Don't skip this step. Your inner fashionista is going to love it. You might feel confident enough already to jump ahead and start trying things on willy-nilly, but I promise you there is a method to my madness, so please follow along. And if you are not feeling confident, then this exercise will help you break out of your shell.

KERRI SCOTT

ROSE-COLORED GLASSES

Begin by putting on an outfit that incorporates the most patterns in your wardrobe possible. The idea is to create a knock-your-socks-off look, so make it as bold and busy a look as you have ever worn. The idea is not to make it look good, *per se*, but rather to push you out of your comfort zone by wearing a combination of your clothes you have never worn before.

This exercise will also help you look at your pile of clothes differently. Because I am asking you to look for patterns, part of your brain will now bring all the patterns to the front of your awareness. Just like if I asked you to find everything in your pile that is red, suddenly, your awareness will be brought to all your red clothing and accessories.

This is a function of your brain called the *reticular activating system* (RAS). I will talk more about the RAS later, so you can continue to look for patterns.

Maybe you have a striped top and floral pants. Combine those with your checkered socks. Yes, even try on your socks and then pair them with some funky shoes. Maybe it is your bikini that has the wildest print or a scarf. I don't care what it is, just put it on and pair it with at least one other print.

If you have a lot of patterns in your wardrobe, try and pick the most outrageous combinations and the boldest colors. If you don't have any patterns in your wardrobe, then pick out the brightest colors and pair them with something you have never worn together.

For most of my readers, this exercise will be something they have never done before.

BUDDHA'S CLOSET

The point is: Don't play it safe in assembling this first outfit. Remember, you want it to be something that pushes you out of our comfort zone.

Go big or go home. You are interrupting your pattern of wearing the same five outfits that you wear day in day out and opening yourself up to new ways of expressing yourself, even if it means expressing something that isn't innately "you" at first. If you must choose between a couple of items, pick the one that feels the most uncomfortable. Not the itchiest sweater uncomfortable, but the print or the color combination that makes you question why you are doing this exercise uncomfortable.

As I write this, I am currently wearing a long-sleeve cheetah print shirt under a short-sleeved paisley print jumper, with my 100 percent alpaca wool geometric patterned vee-neck sweater with bright green, checkered Minecraft creeper socks (which were a hand-me-down from my son) and a burgundy floral print scarf in my hair.

And yes, I am doing this exercise with you. Every step of the way, I am here, supporting you by emptying out my closet and trying things on.

Oops, I forgot to put on some funky shoes, so I will be right back . . . There, now I've got on my Dansko shoes. The ones with the thick, chunky, pink sweater print on them. And let me tell you, I look bizarre. Like the Wicked Witch of the West from *The Wizard of Oz* on a bad mushroom trip.

I can't stop looking at my socks with my shoes because my pants are just the right length to show the two creeper faces on both sides of my calves. This outfit is so terrible it is funny! But that is good, as this is what we are looking for. We should be able to laugh at ourselves, otherwise we wouldn't be having any fun.

Consider taking a photo of your whole outfit, or maybe just a portion of it. Or you may be thinking, *F— that! I am not taking a picture of this* Gong Show. *Let's move on, Kerri!*

But before we try on our next outfit, let's take a moment to pay attention to what emotions are arising. Discomfort, I think, might be at the top of the list (not just because of my itchy alpaca sweater) due to a sense of dread that someone might see you in your outfit.

Oh my God, what if someone were to come to the door at this moment and THIS is what I am wearing. Hell no! I would be horrified. I want to get it off as quickly as I can, but I love this crazy combination of socks and shoes. I feel like an idiot. Nothing about this outfit is flattering. My face looks washed out and pale. I have no waist and the neckline is crying out for some big chunky jewelry to help try and pull it all together. I look like a walking heap of laundry. The only thing that might help is if I put on my funky, coordinating, reading glasses.

It is just as important to have these "Hell no!" moments as it is to be pleased by the outfits we are creating. Our "Hell no!" moments inform our bodies equally, if not more so, than our "Hell yes!" moments. When we begin to recognize what we don't like it is easier for us to recognize what we do like. We are tuning in to our internal guidance system. By paying attention to how our body reacts to certain items of clothing and combinations of clothing together, we attune to our inner voice.

From this first outfit, choose something that you like and keep it on. I am choosing my socks and shoes combination. Everything else can now be put back on the bed. *Thank goodness!*

Speaking of glasses, this is good time to return to the RAS. We are bombarded by information from all our senses, so much so that our brains use this filtering system to limit what information we can process at any given time. It is like wearing a pair of glasses where the shape or color of the lens influences how our mind perceives the world around us.

I am sure you are familiar with the fashion metaphor for an optimistic attitude: *rose-colored glasses.* That tint determines how your mind will interpret a situation or experience or even what someone is saying.

If you wake up and put on your angry glasses, you will notice that breakfast makes you angry, traffic makes you angry, and what your coworker says makes you angry.

Once you realize that you are responsible for which glasses you are wearing, and that these glasses are always changing, you can be empowered to choose the glasses that make the world look best.

SOMETHING BORROWED, SOMETHING BLUE

We are looking for a *Say Yes to the Dress* moment.

"What is that?" you might be asking.

Well, have you ever watched the TLC reality television series *Say Yes to the Dress?* I am obsessed with this show in which experts help a woman who's about to get married find the perfect gown for her ceremony.

Ironically, I never had my own such moment as a bride-to-be because I was determined to design and sew my own wedding dress. But I take great pleasure, nonetheless, in watching the transformation process that happens for each bride as they find "the dress." There is a moment when their entire body language shifts, their facial expression lights up, and everyone watching knows "This is the one!"

Other examples that I recently came across on Facebook are reels from international barber and hairdresser Anthony Claxton and Gue Oliveira. Each video shows the before and after of the client's haircut and color. The results are breathtaking. The elation and pride that each person beams as they see their reflection for the first time is heartwarming. It is like they are seeing their true self for the very first time and it is pure bliss.

So, this is our aim as we change. To have fun and play in our closet until something emerges. There will be a moment when you look in the mirror and say to yourself, *Hello! Where have you been? I want to get to know you. Wink, wink. Let's dance!*

EYES ARE WINDOWS TO THE SOUL

Grab one of the items that you felt a longing toward as you emptied your closet and try it on now.

For me, it was a black silk camisole that my husband gifted me. This camisole is so soft to the touch, and it falls loosely over my torso with delicate, thin straps. It feels like one of those classic pieces that people often wear under a blazer, or sleep in, yet I very rarely put it on.

What could I pair with it, along with these socks and shoes, which might create a fun outfit I would consider wearing? That is the question I am asking myself.

This is when the dance begins. During this process, we are becoming a witness. Watching our reactions, our emotions, all that arises within us as we observe ourselves in the mirror. We are looking at ourselves from every angle as we try on each item of clothing.

Beginning with my black silk camisole, I judge to see how well or poorly it fits. *How do I feel when I put it on? What do I notice when I look in the mirror? Is it loose or is it tight? Does this color suit me?* There are a handful of questions that fill my thoughts and I answer them with each twist and turn in the mirror.

I also put on a pair of mustard yellow hemp pants that I have missed wearing, and again run through a series of questions in my mind. You can use the same ones to assess your responses.

- Does it fit? Is it too tight, too loose? Too long, too short?
- How does it make me feel?
- Do I like this color?
- Am I being critical of myself in this outfit? Or do I like what I see?
- Does this item make me feel like dancing—even just a little?

The answers will come quickly, with just a glance from side to side. Thoughts like, *I don't like wearing the color black. Something about this top doesn't look right. These pants feel uncomfortable, but I love this color yellow.* It is your job to listen to yourself.

Simply allow each thought to arise as you observe your reflection, and even when the voice in your head judges you harshly, be a nonjudgmental witness of the critical thoughts.

Allow yourself to be guided to the next item of clothing by following your best-feeling thoughts. An item may spark a remembrance of something else that's calling to be tried on. Or of a color, a pants length, a texture, or a style. (The process is intuitive.)

I grab my mustard yellow mud cloth scarf to throw over my shoulders. Except the colors don't quite match and the pants no longer fit well. I am practicing discernment. I will get into more detail about what discernment is in a bit, but essentially, I am tuning in to my inner *I like it* or *I don't like it* voice.

This outfit is not a "Hell no!" but nothing about this combination makes me want to keep it on. *The way the length of the pants covers my socks reminds me of a pair of black, raw silk pants that I have never worn. Quick, find them, and put them on. They are high-waisted capris, perfect to show off my fun socks and shoes. My black camisole tucks in nicely to them and with a belt, I can define my waist.*

I'm putting the hemp pants back onto the pile of pants on the bed. *What could I wear under or over my camisole? I have a mauve hand-knit shrug that plays off the colors and textures in my shoes. Oh! I also have a tee-shirt that is a remarkably similar color. I will try that on next . . .* and so it continues. One item leads to the next, which inspires the next.

With each piece you are tuning in and listening to your body, then returning items to the bed that might not be working for you. Don't hold yourself to making any outfit work. Follow your enthusiasm, be led by your curiosity, and simply play. Play with cuffs and layers, scarves and shoes, belts, and bags. Consider clashing colors, coordinating prints, chunky textures, and whatever catches your eye. Ask yourself: *What items could I put together that I never before considered putting together?*

The dance continues, weaving together the process of elimination, your curiosity, a sense of adventure and playfulness. I give you full permission to play in your closet. Try on everything you own. Look in the mirror and admire yourself! Do you remember when you were young, how you would lay out your outfit for the next day? Maybe you played dress up in your friend's grandma's closet, then lip-synced to Madonna.

My dad made me a wooden mannequin I could dress up in my clothes, and I loved doing this. You could have been like me and spent hours drawing and designing clothes in your sketchbook while listening to your George Michael tape on repeat. It is this joy that I rediscover when I clean out my closet.

Don't hang anything up in your closet yet. Just keep trying things on as you feel inspired. Practicing your discernment and listening to your inner voice. Don't take yourself too seriously and don't eliminate anything at this point. This will come later. Allow yourself to be surprised. And have fun!

I want to take a moment here and return to the practice of discernment. There is a mindfulness practice or mantra called *neti neti*, which is Sanskrit for "Not this, not that" or "Not me, not me." When we notice our thoughts focusing on a particularly disturbing story, we tell ourselves about who we are, we can interrupt that thought pattern with the idea "Not me, not me."

For instance, while I am brushing my teeth, I might catch myself thinking, *I am so lazy*, or think, *This laundry room is so disorganized it makes me crazy!* while I am putting clothes in the dryer. But I can stop my train of thought from going any further down the track by internally responding, *Not me, not me.* This mantra helps me remember that while I might have thoughts, I am not these thoughts.

In this process of trying on each item of clothing, we can also bring our awareness to our thoughts. As I mentioned in chapter one, our clothes are a metaphor for our thoughts. In this metaphor, each item of clothing represents a thought we have, and we are learning the practice of discernment.

When we think a thought, we can become a witness to how this thought makes us feel and decide, *Not me, not me* or *Yes me, yes me*. We are moving an internal dialogue of *I like it*, or *I don't like it* outside of ourselves by trying on our thoughts and deciding if they fit us or not.

Ultimately, we are not going to stop thinking but we can curate our thoughts to bring us more joy and even bliss in our daily lives. Okay, back to trying on clothes!

FOLD LIKE A CHEAP SUIT

Watch out for "should" traps, such as assembling outfits that you think society expects you to wear. For instance, I always think I should put together a suitable business look formed by pairing black dress pants with a crisp white shirt and a black blazer.

Sure, I will try this on next, but after I do, I must be honest with myself whether it is something I will feel good wearing. It may simply be something I think I *should* wear. But maybe I can pair one of those items with something else and express myself more craftily.

Try on your "should" outfits, and then play with them so they don't keep you boxed in. What would be a different and more interesting way of creating this look with what you have on your bed?

> *I've always found that a crisp-collared pure white shirt doesn't suit me. The pure white color is not a good match for my skin tone. But what if, instead of a black blazer, I wear my hand-knit, chunky, sleeveless, cream-colored wool sweater over top? I like the way those pieces come together. Or instead of the collared white shirt, what if I lower the neckline and try a white eyelet top under my black blazer? This works better too.*

As you rearrange and recombine, keep thinking about how to include pieces you wouldn't normally consider. Remember you are the only one judging you. No one else is watching. You can do anything! There are no rules. You are the artist crafting your masterpiece.

Hey, maybe you want to grab that Pearl Jam tee-shirt out of your partner's wardrobe and try that on under your blazer? Or what about a neon hoodie under a blazer? The options are endless.

DRESSED TO THE NINES

As you follow the inspiration from item to item, you will slowly see a new version of yourself when you look in your mirror. It comes as pleasing colors, flattering necklines, complimentary shapes, and interesting textures. Your inner critic will quiet down and you will begin to fall in love with yourself. Your perceived flaws will be masked by the cut and drape of the clothes, and when you look in the mirror, in your head you will hear yourself saying, *I want to know more about that person!*

As you feel this happening with your outfit, like on *Say Yes to the Dress*, it is time to "jack it up." Grab a pair of shoes and some jewelry, or maybe a hat or a scarf. Add whatever will take this outfit from "I like it" to "Hell yes!"

SIX

RETAIL THERAPY

"You are not your body. You are actually an extension of the power that created the whole universe." [6]

RUPAUL

When you find an outfit that lights you up, you need to celebrate! You need to embody this "Hell yes!" feeling. It isn't necessarily because of the combination of clothes that you put on, though it may seem that way because everything else before this outfit didn't spark the same feelings of well-being. Really, these sensations of joy are coming from within you, and it is important to pause and celebrate that you are the source of these good feelings.

STEP 5: CELEBRATE

So, here you are. You are pausing, looking at yourself in the mirror. Ask yourself what you are feeling. Warm? Relaxed? Joyful? Giddy? Impressed? Pleased? Excited? Love? Adoration?

As I moved away from my dress pants and blazer, and after some royal blue corduroy, knits, and kaftans, I eventually wandered into a pair of hemp overalls I designed. That first sense of myself began to appear. Something about the rolled-up hems and the loose cut of the overalls was appealing to me.

I fussed with what belonged underneath it or over it and was called to a khaki green tank top. This surprised me because I had been so sensitive about showing my arms earlier in this process. But what I saw in my reflection encouraged me. My arms appeared fit and there was a strength in them that I had not been able to see before.

Next, I grabbed a cute, short, puffy sleeved cashmere cardigan and was at once taken by the deep neckline. It cinched under my bust with four buttons to create an emperor waistline that flattered me. This was hidden under the overalls, so I dug out my beige, Dhoti-style velour pants. The material of these is draped and gathered in such a way that it falls like a waterfall over my hips and narrows at my ankles. I absolutely adore the cut of these pants and have the best intentions to make more but never do. In my reflection, I emerged. I swayed from side to side, swinging my hips. The gathered sleeves and the draped pants created a remarkably interesting silhouette. One that I am not accustomed to seeing. All in a neutral and natural palette.

To "jack" myself up, I slipped into my slouchy leather ankle boots. Oh, how they complemented all the draping!

Now I may never wear this outfit out of my house, but I can't deny that I want to keep looking at myself in the mirror and spend more time with the person I see when I have them on. My reflection invokes certain sensations in me. I feel empowered and sensual. There is a sense of royalty that bubbles up, maybe because my husband and I are currently watching the prequel to *Game of Thrones*. I want to admire myself, put my hands on my hips, and sway. I feel exotic, like a genie.

Ask yourself, *Where do I feel this well-being in my body?* Close your eyes. Can you still feel it? Are there tingles in your extremities? In your core? Do you feel more confident? Has your posture changed? Can you make those sensations feel more expansive by bringing your awareness to them? Is there a certain song that this outfit begs for? I highly encourage you to put it on and dance in front of the mirror!

Of course, given what I'm wearing, the song that sprang to mind for me was Christina Aguilera's "Genie in a Bottle." Which immediately made me laugh. It was perfect for the outfit. And yet, there was a time when I had to lip-synch this song without knowing the words at all. I worked at Club Med Turquoise as a costume designer. All staff members, particularly those on the entertainment team, were strongly encouraged to take part in the nightly productions along with the guests.

I'll never forget how our choreographer decided one night that I looked like Christina Aguilera and sent me out on stage. My confidence in the new outfit I assembled far surpasses any I had back then, and even now, twenty some odd years later, it feels good showing off my belly button while I dance for myself.

Take a photo of yourself in your new outfit even if only you will ever see it. If you're feeling bold, post it on social media. You may want this image to pop up occasionally and remind you of the feeling of well-being you had when you liked how you looked. Remember to use #buddhascloset to tag your photo so I can see how you look too.

This is a great time to write in your journal about what you are experiencing if journaling is something you love to do.

BEAUTY IS ONLY SKIN DEEP

Just like those moments in the before-and-after reels that I am enjoying watching so much on social media, you have experienced a transformation. There is a distinct moment when what is and appears to be wholly external is a recognition of an inner knowing. This is the state that I discussed in chapter one, where your sense of fulfillment first appears to be from the clothing you are wearing, but truly it is originating within you.

What possibly began as self-doubt, judgmental thoughts and harsh self-criticism has turned into self-acceptance and even self-love. You are breaking free of your inner critic and no longer identify with its judgmental thoughts. You feel joyful and revere your appearance. You are beautiful as you are in your body.

There is a moment of prolonged self-love that flickers in the eyes of every person who loves themself in their attire. Let this positive regard and admiration spark a song in your heart that moves your soul to the front of your awareness.

It may seem at first glance that it is your clothing and accessories that create this sudden and deep appreciation you have for yourself, but to recreate this outfit another day might not have the same blossoming effect. It is all in this moment of beautiful realization.

The soul emerges when we allow ourselves to show up in a completely different way than usual. In new clothes that have been jacked up.

Ideas of who you think you should be and what you think you should look like disappear. In jacked-up clothing, you will recognize yourself but without any of the conditioned beliefs and thoughts about your appearance that shaped who you were before.

This exercise is fun because when you do it you get to completely reinvent yourself, inside and out. It helps you recognize that you can reinvent yourself anytime with or without clothing. You are free.

This is success. The feeling of success is also the feeling of well-being. It feels like a sense of aliveness and a connection with something deeper. It is love, and you created it all on your own. Within you.

This moment, with this outfit is unique. When you wear these clothes again you may not have this same sensation because it is not the clothes that are making you feel great. The external fulfillment that we were once seeking from our clothing is replaced by an internal fulfillment.

But the real secret is that you can create a good feeling within you whenever you want. Now that you know what it feels like and that you did it, you can summon well-being for yourself in the shower, while walking the dog, or as you're drinking your morning tea.

Stay as long as you like in the outfit you created. Truly embrace who you are. Embody all the beautiful sensations of recognition and remembrance of who you are as they are emerging.

LIFE IS A MIRROR

Now, stay with me here. I am going to do a deep dive into Buddhist philosophy; or more specifically, into yogic philosophy and Vedanta. In the Preface, I talked about "trying on" various modalities. Well, the one tradition that felt like it fit me like a glove when I tried it on was that of Advaita Vedanta, and it looked good on me!

Although it can be complex to explain, simply put, the philosophy of Advaita Vedanta is based on the concept of *nonduality*. Philosophically, this means that the essence of everything in the world is oneness. I liked the way its practices made me feel compared to those of many other spiritual modalities I tried. When I first read about it, I thought, *This reflects me. This is who I am.* just like my outfit sparked my desire to want to know more about who this person is that I saw in the mirror.

Advaita Vedanta answered the ultimate question of who I am in a way that has prompted me to continue to seek her out repeatedly. Day after day. It is the modality that I enjoy reading about the most and I keep the yogic philosophy as part of my daily practice.

In a YouTube video I watched, Michael Singer, author of *The Untethered Soul*, tells a metaphorical story about the experience of trying on clothes while shopping.

Singer says:

When you are standing in front of those mirrors, a very fascinating, deep thing is happening. Taking in the reflection of what you are seeing and letting it process through your entire judgment system, through your heart, through your senses of feeling, trying to see how it moves you.

And if your heart opens, you feel warm and you feel good about it. You say I like it. But this is a lie. What you really like is the feeling that you felt come up inside. Not the outfit. That outfit that made you feel that way today, may hang in that closet for years and never get worn again, because it never feels right again.[7]

What he is describing is the feeling of well-being that we like. We associate this feeling of well-being with the clothes that we put on. We mistakenly believe that it is the clothing that is bringing us this sensation of fulfillment and joy, and we condition ourselves to believe that we need certain clothes to find that feeling again. We mistakenly attach our feeling of well-being (which is inherent to us) to our clothes, which are always changing.

Seeking good feelings is the motivation behind "retail therapy." It feels good at the time we find and purchase a new outfit—getting a dopamine hit for our effort—but the joy doesn't last. And it is not just clothes that we do this with. We attach to objects, careers, people, food, social media, thoughts, emotions, and ideas—things which, again, are always changing.

Buddhists call this the *root of suffering*, our misplaced belief that our well-being comes from something that is changing. When in fact, our well-being truly originates from our awareness of that which is unchanging. Like in Buddhist philosophy, yogic philosophy describes the unchanging Self or the Self as eternal. Both traditions recognize that to stop our suffering, we must come to know that which is unchanging. We must observe the impermanence of everything with the one thing that is permanent, our awareness.

This is the unchanging Self that I referred to in the Preface. It is who we are, and we feel a great sense of happiness and joy when we recognize ourselves as this.

The you that you see in the mirror is always changing. Your clothing is changing, your hair is changing, your skin is changing, your body is changing, your personality is changing. How then, going back to the example of my pink corduroy pants, could I know that those pants were so quintessentially me if I am always changing? Well, they aren't me. The experience of finding them was simply retail therapy.

I thought I would feel better if I had them—so much so that even my friends came to believe these pants embodied my well-being. Even months after purchasing them, a sense of joy still arises within me when I see them in my closet. But given enough time, that joy will fade and be replaced by joy in something else. Perhaps another item of clothing, or a pair of shoes.

You and I both know that these pants will not stop me from aging. They will not end the suffering I feel when I judge myself as unhealthy or too old, too weak, or unattractive.

BUDDHA'S CLOSET

Only by realizing that all the parts of me are constantly changing can I step back and find comfort in knowing that the witness of all that is changing is my unchanging Self. This is the purpose of the practice of deliberate self-love, knowing that who we truly are is unchanging.

BIRTHDAY SUIT

We are exploring the unchanging Self as we play in the Self that is changing. By recognizing what is always changing, we come to discover what (or who) is unchanging. In our closets, this is a literal example of a metaphor that has been taught an infinite number of ways.

We can say that everything is our guru. A mountain, water, the air, and more. We are pure and free. We are not the clothes that we wear. We are not the thoughts that we think. We are not the emotions that we feel. We experience each of these, but we return to our pure and free selves when we recognize that underneath all that changes within us and around us exists that which is unchanging.

To be clear, returning to our pure selves doesn't mean wearing nothing at all, just acknowledging that our bodies, our figures, our shape and size, and our skin are all changing. These forms are "outfits" being "worn" by that which is unchanging—the true Self. And we can play with the possibilities the forms afford us.

We can change our hairstyle, our hair color, our makeup, and our nail polish, as well as our sleeping and eating habits. These are all playful ways of changing our appearance or our mood, but none changes that which is unchanging. The true Self.

Ultimately, by recognizing the unchanging Self, you will be able also to recognize everything that is changing. You are none of these things. You are not your clothes. You are not your body. You are not your mind. You are not your thoughts. You are not your emotions. You are not your beliefs. You are not your ideas.

Neti, neti.

Again, as my satsang teacher, Hirdaya, says: "You are unchanging, forever free, and pure." Hopefully, the steps in the remaining chapters will help you become more familiar with this new recognition of yourself.

SEVEN

MAYA

"Your personal style and your style in general can change all the time because you're always changing." [8]

SARA CAMPOSARCONE

The next three chapters will shine a light on the relationship between your thoughts and your clothes. You will be putting some of your clothes back in your closet, storing others, and clearing some out to create a seasonal wardrobe, but you will also be challenging your beliefs about what you can and cannot wear.

STEP 6: CREATE

I want to give you some tools to help you identify what pieces you want to include in your wardrobe selection, such as the three-word method that I will describe in a little bit, which is advocated by wardrobe stylist Allison Bornstein whom I admire.[9] I also want you to begin to question your beliefs about your clothing as an expression of your identity.

Typically, clothing is an outward expression of who we are. Clothes are viewed as a form of communication to the world, telling anyone who sees us something about our identity, our personality, and our preferences. But as you learned in the last chapter, who you are is unchanging! The clothes we wear are simply representations of all that is changing.

And what is changing? Your body, your mind, your personality, your moods, your career, your emotions, your age, your interests, your desires, and on and on it goes. So, the clothing you decide to wear can be a representation of any of these changing aspects of yourself.

This is where creating a seasonal wardrobe gets fun. You can playfully experiment with the parts of you that are changing to create a new outward identity just because you can! You are building confidence in yourself as unchanging. And when you know that you are your unchanging Self, the changing self gets to be anyone and everyone.

So, how do you take the pile of clothing you've taken out of your closet and plopped on your bed (or near your bed) and sort through it to create your seasonal wardrobe? At this point, nothing should be hanging in your closet, which is immaculately clean. Nothing is put away. It is time to do the busy work and start curating and eliminating.

Since clothing no longer represents us—because we are unchanging—we need to come up with some constraints to help guide our artistic process. I like the word *constraint* because it is lingo I picked up from my studies in industrial design. It is not restrictive or confining in the physical sense.

Constraints are simply a few words that can help guide our vision of the new identity we are playing with and curious about. Where these words come from can be intentional or intentionally unintentional. For example, we might take our constraint words from a deck of angel cards. Angel cards were a modality that caught my interest early on my spiritual journey, and these could be playfully used to decide on a few descriptive words.

The three-word method that I mentioned earlier is another great example of giving ourselves constraints. Developed by Allison Bornstein, it acts like a checklist to help us decide what to keep or purge from our closet. By choosing three words that define our personal style, we can use them as a guide when selecting outfits. Each outfit should hold some element of all three words.

WALK A MILE IN THEIR SHOES

Words can mean different things to different people. They evoke emotions and reactions. An old belief is that our clothing symbolizes our identity. *Blue collar* and *stuffed shirt* are cultural symbols of certain career or personality choices that many people have made.

But can we examine for a minute how clothing creates our identity? I know, for instance, that I walk differently in combat boots than I do in heels. My whole attitude changes, as I feel more confident or chunky. I want to assume space, to feel heavier and present—and to exude power.

Likewise, when I wear pearls, I often feel like I am an imposter. I love them, they are my favorite gem (if we can call pearls *gemstones*); however, I don't feel pure enough, innocent enough, or highbred enough to pull them off in a believable way.

I have some subconscious beliefs around what it means to wear combat boots versus pearls that were taught to me by my culture and society.

Wearing certain colors can affect our moods. Yellow and blue are said to be mood boosters while black or brown can bring us down.

Colors can also have certain meanings, and we believe that when we wear them, those qualities adhere to our being. On a symbolic level, black is often viewed as sophisticated, for example. On the other hand, white symbolizes purity and innocence. Red lace is viewed as sexy. These symbolic beliefs seem infinite, but they are an illusion.

In Sanskrit, *maya* is the term for any belief that who we are is defined by any quality that is always changing. But all the beliefs and personalities that emerge are being witnessed by a single unchanging Self. Just as we change our clothes, we can change our beliefs.

OFF THE CUFF

In the previous chapter, you crafted a "Hell yes!" look. Now, can you come up with three words that describe this outfit? Mine (for my genie pants outfit) would be *draping, romantic,* and *exotic.* Ironically, I don't think any of my family or friends would use these same words to describe either me or how I typically dress. Yet, these words begin to embody the sense of well-being I felt when I saw my unchanging Self in my reflection.

Your words could include a color, a texture, or a sound. Maybe the word *texture* or *sound* itself will be one of your words. Your self-description could include the name of a place or a person, a feeling, or an action. There are no restrictions, choose whichever words hold special meaning for you.

Ideally, these words will become symbolic of your spirituality; they will serve as reminders that you are unchanging.

It is officially time to undress and hang up this jacked-up outfit that makes you feel great—the one that gave you your "Hell yes!" —in your pristine closet. This is also a good time to collect any clean laundry that you started earlier in this process and add it to your piles.

ACE UP YOUR SLEEVE

Start the whole exercise over. The next few outfits should be easy to collate and integrate back into your wardrobe. If you're like me, a beautiful sense of well-being will rise within you, and your clothes will simply become a reflection of this inner state.

Guide yourself to choose clothing for your wardrobe that evokes these qualities. It is time to get curious and find more items of clothing and more outfits that, in some big or subtle way, incorporate your three words. It should only get more fun as you find new, exciting, and unlikely combinations that you love, all the while sustaining the inherent sense of well-being that you discovered. Your new style is emerging.

This time as you are trying various items continue asking yourself discerning questions like, "Does this item of clothing physically fit the body shape I currently have?" It makes sense that this is one of the first leading questions you ask yourself when you try anything on. Followed by, "Is it too long or too short? Do I like this color? Is this in season?" And "Is it damaged?"

You can set aside the items that you know for certain won't be incorporated into your seasonal wardrobe because they're ill-fitting. Also set aside items that are damaged or need mending or alterations. We will circle back to these in chapter nine.

As we discussed in step one, Clarify, maybe you are curious to explore a different part of your wardrobe or a different type of wardrobe all together. Is there an item of clothing that you want to wear more often? Or maybe a shirt that still has the tags on it is something that will inspire you to build an outfit around it. If it is our intention to be more organized or to declutter our closets in this process, we are no longer seeking fulfillment solely from achieving this goal because we have already achieved fulfilment through our unchanging Self.

I am setting the intention this season to find more ways to wear my wool camel coat and the color yellow. To my delight, through this process, I considered wearing them together, which is something I never would have done before. I discovered a whole new look that I love by combining neutrals and colors. I can pair this coat with all sorts of colors. Not only yellow (sweatpants with a naturally dyed flannel infinity scarf), but hot pink (my corduroy pants and cable knit neck tube), and baby blue (wide-leg denim pants with a long wool scarf). Giving myself permission to wear my $400 coat with my $10 sweatpants was the key to this playful discovery. Any beliefs I might have held about what I am allowed to wear are unravelling as I change my clothes.

THINKING CAP

Returning to the central metaphor that our closet is our mind and our clothes are our thoughts, please remember that as we curate our clothes we can also curate our thoughts.

It is a well-known fact that as human beings we have a negativity bias. It is a normal tendency to perceive events and situations as negative and dwell on these cons, as though we are wearing "negativity glasses" instead of rose-colored glasses. In order to overcome this bias in relation to your thoughts, your next step will be to come up with constraints for your mind.

Three types of thought constraint that have a proven effect of improving our overall well-being are affirmations, gratitude, and presence. We can create affirmations to counter negative thoughts we repeat to ourselves. For instance, if we were to think, *I am going to fail*, we could choose to replace this thought with the affirmation "Everything always works out for me."

Gratitude is an intentional practice of being thankful for what is present in your life. If we witnessed ourselves complaining, *My house is too small*, then we could mindfully or literally make a list of all the reasons we love our home.

Lastly, presence is a moment-by-moment awareness of what is happening now. When we observe that we are stuck in a thought about the past or having anxiety about the future, we can practice bringing our awareness to our bodies. What sensations are we having? What are we seeing, hearing, touching, smelling, or even tasting? By noticing what is present, we can quiet our thoughts.

We will continue this discussion about our clothing as thoughts and the skeletons that might be hiding in our closets in the next chapter.

EIGHT

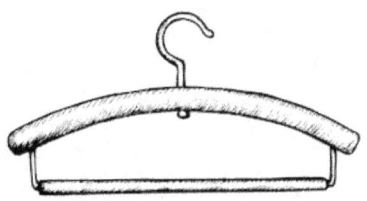

SOLE SEARCHING

Why did the mirror go to school?
To learn how to reflect on itself.

As I have said before, the pile of clothes you've heaped on your bed during this clearing out and putting back process represent an accumulation of your thoughts and beliefs about your identity. And when we bring our awareness to our thoughts, we must learn to exercise discernment over which thoughts we allow ourselves to think. Just like the practice of discernment or neti neti we used to create our "Hell yes!" moment, we can decide if we like a thought or don't like a thought.

STEP 7: CONTEMPLATE

Looking in my sock drawer is like looking at the ghosts of Christmases past. This most recent Christmas, I received a pair of lovely green wool socks that I adore from my sister-in-law. They are so incredibly comfortable and the shade of green matches one of my go-to tee-shirts, which makes them perfect for color blocking, something I love doing lately. The last Christmas I spent with my parents, my sister gave me a pair of super-funky pink snowboarding socks complete with hibiscus flowers and palm fronds. Then there are the socks I got from Santa (aka my husband), my mother-in-law, or my mom, which include a vast selection of merino wool, pink stripes, Indigenous designs, and cashmere.

At one point in the last fifteen years, I tried to coordinate my socks, on advice from my father-in-law, into one monotone collection. I went out and bought multiple pairs of matching black dress socks. His theory was that it would never matter if a sock were lost in the laundry because its "other half" would have numerous other sole mates to keep it company. But over the years I have been gifted so many other interesting socks that his system has fallen out of favor with me.

Most recently, there has been an influx of hand-me-down socks from my son that he donates to me because he rapidly grows out of everything. I will talk more about hand-me-downs in a bit, but if you recall from reading chapter three and as you were emptying your closet, you may notice certain memories arising in connection with certain items of clothes. You were so excited to buy some pants, but you regret buying others. Certain items may have made you feel bad that you haven't worn them, whereas others might have reminded you of certain people. It is these items of clothing that lead us to contemplate.

BUDDHA'S CLOSET

SKELETONS IN OUR CLOSET

If your closet is symbolic of your mind, which thoughts do you want to allow into your mind? And which clothes do you want to put back in your closet? Think of contemplating these questions as a kind of meditation.

As we discussed in chapter one, the most effective way to bring our awareness to our thoughts is through meditation, but as I mentioned earlier, just like with cleaning, the first step to meditation often is not wanting to do it. Meditation can be a difficult first step to take.

Looking at your clothing, what parts of your identity have you been holding on to without your awareness of them? And what thoughts have inadvertently shaped your identity?

By now, you might already see how the practice of creating a seasonal wardrobe is like a meditation. Item by item, keep noticing what thoughts arise as you sort through, try on, and get ready to put your clothing back into the closet.

We are well past the difficult first step and already deep into step seven of the eight-fold process. We have finished clarity, clearing, cleaning, changing, celebrating, and creating and now we are contemplating our clothing.

If you are going to "pay" attention to your thoughts or invest money in new clothes, they may as well be clothes that you love. Clothes that light you up or, as organizer extraordinaire Marie Kondo says, *spark joy* in you. She coined this phrase.

Clothes represent thought forms. Or certain thought forms are attached to certain clothes. Specific clothing holds specific memories. They may remind of you of a person, like my many Christmas socks remind me of the people who gave them to me;

or they may remind you of a time, a place, or an experience. So, it is beneficial to ask yourself, *How does this memory make me feel? Is this a feeling I want to put back into my closet? Or can I replace this item with a different item of clothing that doesn't carry that same weight of thought attached to it? Can I pick something to wear that holds no attachment whatsoever or even makes me feel good about myself?* If you find a certain item of clothing bringing up unpleasant memories or thoughts, set this aside and don't add it to your seasonal wardrobe.

This process of curating clothing is where you make your happiness the priority when choosing an outfit. This is similar in many ways to the contemporary trend of *dopamine dressing*. Often color plays a huge role in dopamine dressing because of how colors can influence our moods. But comfort plays a significant part as well. Things like temperature and fit are important considerations for overall comfort curation.

A key to happiness is to choose clothing that doesn't become an annoyance or distraction. Even sound and smell can contribute to how happy our clothing makes us feel. Certain sounds invoke pleasure, and some scents can bring back favorable memories or remind us to be present.

I have a pair of earrings that are made from naturally cured moose hide. They are deliciously smoky and when I wear them, their scent wafts in and out of my awareness. Wearing them is a sensual experience that brings my attention to the present moment.

BUDDHA'S CLOSET

SOMETHING TO HANG YOUR HAT ON

Just like a belief, an outfit we wear repeatedly is simply a thought we keep thinking. Often, our beliefs do not even belong to us. Going back to the matter of hand-me-downs, we adopt our beliefs from the people around us.

When I emerged from the fog of maternal sleep deprivation (which for me lasted the first three months of my children's lives), I realized that all the clothes in my closet had been given to me by either my mom or my sister. I had not chosen a single item by myself. And for someone whose identity has been wrapped up in fashion for most of her life, this was a shocking discovery. Nothing felt like mine.

And just like our beliefs, there are so many beliefs about what we should or should not wear that have been given to us by society.

Any time we believe we should do something we feel an enormous pressure to obey. But rules like "Don't wear white after Labor Day" or one I currently see trending "Don't wear socks with sandals," are oppressive. Then there's my favorite: "You can't wear pink and red together." I break this rule often, as I sit here in my red plaid pants and fluorescent pink hoodie.

It is a good practice to challenge societal beliefs if they don't make us happy.

There may be items in our closets that have been passed down to us, and these might have held such value to the person that they came from that we cannot imagine letting them go—either for fear of disappointing the person that gave something to us or for fear of letting ourselves down in some way. We attach the memory we hold dear to the item, and we fear losing the memory by getting rid of the item.

This takes us back to the root of suffering, like we talked about in chapter six. We attach to objects, careers, people, food, social media, thoughts, emotions, and ideas. Things that, again, are always changing. This is our misplaced belief that our well-being comes from these objects. When in fact, our well-being originates from our awareness of that which is unchanging.

If we are hanging on to an item out of fear, we are attaching to an emotion, which is changing. But when we know that we are unchanging, we can become witnesses to these emotions and let them go.

An item might lose the sentimental value it originally carried. Sentimental attachment can swing both ways. Either we keep a thing forever, even if we never wear it, or we want to get rid of it at once because the emotional attachment or corresponding trauma is too much.

SKIRT AROUND THE ISSUE

This leads to another good question to contemplate: *What am I intentionally excluding from my closet?*

What we don't wear can often reveal unhealthy thoughts and habits, anxiety, trauma, and other issues that we are avoiding.

I own few dresses and skirts, and this has almost always been the case. I have never felt particularly comfortable in either.

Maybe my lack of dresses and skirts stem from dress trauma that I experienced as a child. My elementary school was a teaching school for a university. In every classroom, there was an overhead viewing gallery. Teaching students would occasionally visit to create a semi-secret audience hidden behind large, dark looming windows. In one of my first gym classes in kindergarten, we practiced various activities under the watchful eyes of some university students. Blue gym mats lined the floor as we barrel-rolled and somersaulted. I happened to be wearing a dress on this day. Each time I put my hands above my head and rolled to the right or rolled to the left as instructed, my dress would roll up with me, showing my underwear to everyone in the gallery. I felt exposed and helpless to make it stop. Easier never to wear dresses or skirts again to feel safe.

This is an example of how my past is affecting the decisions I make in the present. It is how I have attached meaning to something changing, in this case my sense of security. But now that I know I am unchanging, I can drop this attachment, after which I could set an intention to add more dresses and skirts into my wardrobe over time. Or not. Either way, I will be at peace.

A fashion *faux pas* can create lasting trauma. It might sound silly to say, but I bet you can think of a time when you might have been experimenting with a new trend only to receive less-than-favorable feedback or even harsh criticism. Perhaps your skirt got tucked under your backpack at college and you walked through campus with only your nylons covering your bum.

In high school, I religiously watched *Fashion Television*. In one runway show, models in fishnet tights wore denim cutoffs and brightly colored tee-shirts. I figured I could take this look and translate it into streetwear. Which meant I could wear an oversized orange tee-shirt, shorts, and fishnet tights to school. I felt like I was on the forefront of fashion until some snarky girls in my class made some comments about my outfit. Or maybe it was the boys saying something inappropriate about the fishnets that tore me down emotionally. Or both.

I played it safe after that fashion experiment. Clothing became something to hide behind rather than draw attention to myself with. This subconscious fear of being seen still surprises me on occasion, particularly when I push myself out of my comfort zone, like braiding wool dreadlock extensions into my hair. I absolutely love how they look and how they make me feel at home but wearing them out in public causes me to summon a level of courage into which I don't often tap. They make me challenge my belief about caring what other people think of me.

Honestly, it doesn't matter what other people will think about you in an outfit, but your thoughts about what you think other people will think about you matter if those opinions make you feel uncomfortable or somehow constrained.

DON'T GET YOUR KNICKERS IN A KNOT

I believe looking at our intimate garments reveals our deep, core beliefs. When we are almost naked and standing in front of a mirror, it's common to think, *I am not enough*. This may be the greatest little lie any of us will tell ourselves. And this is rarely a one-and-done thought. It is a subtle and pervasive thought that's almost, or entirely, subconscious. We identify so deeply with this thought in all its forms that we wear it like underwear.

The thought *I am not enough* can be worn so close to our skin that it is almost unseen. In my experience, many of us say this thought so quietly or with such conviction that we don't dare question it. We are comfortable being uncomfortable until it begs for our attention, and then it begins to feel like a wedgie that we need to pick out of our ass. Most of the time it's like a loose underwire in your bra that you tolerate because you have gotten used to it although it is constantly poking you.

We take these four little words—I am not enough—and dress them up with other words. *I am not good enough. I am not smart enough. I am not pretty enough.* And on and on it goes. These types of thoughts are the last to be recognized before we see the unchanging Self. These are the last thoughts we take off before we stand naked and happy before ourselves.

The history of underwear is ripe with oppression, constriction, and conformity, therefore I recommend, particularly if this is the first time you have cleaned out your closet using the Buddha's Closet method, to save sorting your underwear for another day.

We tend to wear them more than any other item of clothing we own, which, on a per-wear basis, makes them the most sustainable items in our closet. And we tend to have categories of undergarments, which in part depends on who, if anyone, is going to see them other than us. Period panties, sports bras, padded bras, wireless bras, push-up bras, sexy lingerie, grandma panties, long underwear, and big girl panties are just a few of many variations of intimates in our closet.

When it comes to organizing your underwear drawer, sort and fold your intimates as you put them away. Don't hesitate to throw something out no matter what sort of attachment you have to it. It could be handmade out of the softest bamboo fabric, but if it is worn out and over stretched now, then it is time to let it go. And don't hesitate to invest in good, durable underwear.

Spend money on underwear that makes you feel comfortable. These are the items of clothing you wear the most.

BOYFRIEND SWEATER

Another form of attachment, which is a kind of thought trap that I have fallen into in the past, was hanging on to items of clothing that romanticized ideals of who I wanted to be when I forgot that I am unchanging. (I will talk more about why we forget we are unchanging in the next chapter.) I am quite the fantasist. I have quite a few clothing items that live in my sewing room. Not to mention hordes of fabric I hang on to with the idea of a certain design locked into my imagination. I fantasize about remaking and dip-dying these clothes, getting crafty and wearing them or selling them. But in all honestly, I love thinking about these ideas more than I like being crafty.

All your contemplation is very much like pulling on a loose thread. The more you pull on it the more you can expect your "sweater" to unravel. Expect that feelings of grief may arise when you decide to let something go. You formed a relationship with that item, whether you remember buying it from a local designer or associate wearing it with a special memory and it has become a part of your identity.

Cleaning out your mental closet is like having your identity come undone. Sometimes we need to undo everything we think we know about ourselves to know we are not any of those things. This is your big opportunity to release everything you think defines you.

You have been diligently going through your clothes, item by item, sensing if you want to try them on, hang them in your closet, put them away in storage, or let them go. When do you know enough is enough? When nothing else inspires you.

You might reach a point where your closet feels complete and none of the remaining clothes on your bed call to you. If so, stop.

In doing my own closet makeover, I reached a good balance of bright colors and neutrals. I included some exotic prints and lots of puffy sleeved shirts. Enough was enough for me at that point. My closet was meticulously organized and uncluttered.

Next, I will conclude my eight-fold process. This is the step when I get rid of unloved or ill-fitting items. So, when you reach a stage where you are feeling good about what is in your closet and you still have a pile of clothing on your bed, this next step will help you sort through these last remaining items.

NINE

SADHANA

She wears her heart on her sleeve.

Remaining are all the items that do not meet your self-identified constraints. With everything that is left on your bed or collection space, there are a few questions remaining that will help you wrap up your closet cleanout. Questions about lifestyle and values. Each item can be checked against the following criteria to determine if it will be put in your closet, into storage, or discarded. Once you have made these decisions and formed a discard pile, we will discuss a variety of options as to how to get rid of these items.

STEP 8: CONCLUDE

The criteria for working with your remaining clothes are lifestyle, fit, condition, season, and preference.

Let's first consider the issue of lifestyle. Do you need certain or specific clothes for your work? Certain clothes for exercising in? Certain clothes for sleeping?

When I examined the contents of my own laundry bin, I discovered that 15 percent of my dirty clothes were work clothes. I have a few pairs of dedicated pants—scrub pants and hemp pants with lots of deep pockets—that I only wear when I am doing commercial cleaning. I pair these with a tee-shirt and a zip-up fleece jacket. It is a self-imposed uniform of sorts. The outfit that works the best for the type of work that I do.

Return anything to your closet that you need for the lifestyle activities you have identified.

At this point you may have set aside items that no longer fit. Fit is important, however most of us tend to gloss over a poor fit and go into denial when something we like the look of is uncomfortable. We also make excuses and allowances for garments we have fond memories of wearing just to keep certain items in our closet.

When we are working like nonattached Buddhas in cleaning out our closets, part of the process is to acknowledge openly that each item of clothing stands for a conscious or unconscious thought we have. And then we strive to make peace with the thought, so we can build greater self-acceptance while also letting go of clothing that doesn't fit.

I have an entire bin of clothing that I love which no longer fits. My rationale for keeping these items is that I am holding on to them for my tween daughter to grow into. Because this is the reason, I am choosing to pack them carefully in a storage box to honor my choice.

BUDDHA'S CLOSET

If you do not have the desire or the storage space to keep clothes that no longer fit, move them into your discard pile.

Now, we need to address the items that we noticed had condition issues. They may have been ripped, torn, stained, or frayed. We are coming out of a societal phase where we were too quick to throw something out if it was damaged or stained. It was often easier and less expensive simply to replace an item of clothing than to take the time to repair it. There is beautiful resurgence of mending and altering, or repurposing, clothing.

As I mentioned before, I had a brief career as a fashion designer taking vintage clothes and repurposing them into new fashion. Now, on social media I see this happening increasingly, as a trend, and I find it thrilling.

How does our relationship change with an item of clothing if we take the time to sew a patch over a hole or shorten a hem that is too long? Will we reach for that item more often if we put the extra care and time into repairing and altering it? If mending and alterations are your values, then you can put these items on your to do list. But if repairing clothing doesn't appeal to you, with gratitude, release damaged items and put them with your other discards.

Some items may be out of season and therefore can get stored for when they will be useful. Personally, it is fun to find ways to wear summer clothes in the winter. For example, I have a hot pink beach coverup with turquoise pompoms on it that matches my pink pants so well that, if I layer it over a warm sweater, it can be a super fun monochromatic addition to my winter wardrobe. Any items that are too warm for summer or too cold for winter can be put away for another seasonal wardrobe.

Lastly, there are also items that, as my daughter says, "I don't really wear anymore, and they are really annoying." Preference is the final criteria for determining when to let something go. If you know in your heart you are never going to wear something again, thank it and move it to your discard pile.

As your internal Buddha handles and assesses your clothes, some items may show up as a "Hell no!" simply based on how they make you feel. Speaking personally, I no longer accept that leggings need to be a part of my wardrobe. It took me many years to allow myself this broad elimination. The truth is, every time I wear legging, my legs get so itchy and uncomfortable that I am instantly transported back to my childhood when I would wear tights. The crotch would droop, and the ankles would bunch up, and I wanted to crawl out of my skin with how scratchy every part of me felt.

I don't know if everyone feels this way in tights or if it was due in part to my chronically dry skin, but by midlife I finally recognized that I never had to feel this uncomfortable again—no matter what the trends were.

THROWING IN THE TOWEL

There are so many options for how to discard of clothing and the end of a closet cleanout is an opportunity to tune in to your values. If certain items are in good repair, you can decide whether you prefer to take them to a local consignment store, sell them online on sites like Poshmark or Facebook Marketplace, participate in a clothing swap, give them to a friend, or donate them to a thrift store. It might be important to you to consider if there is a certain business or organization that aligns with your values which you would like to support when you consign or donate used clothing. Or when an item is damaged, before simply throwing it out, it may be important to you to find out if the company who made it has a clothing recycling program. A much-beloved article of clothing will one day need to be discarded or the fabric recycled, which is a relatively recent option that the fashion industry is leaning in to more and more. Finally, can you use this item of clothing as a rag and get another type of use out of it before it is disposed of?

The thoughts that we choose not to keep may not be as easy to dispose of. They have a way of coming back into our minds, often when we are triggered, or feeling defensive. But they also reappear in our day-to-day activities. This becomes our *sadhana*, a practice to continually bring our awareness to our thoughts and choose, moment by moment, which thoughts we put our attention on and which thoughts we let go.

BIG SHOES TO FILL

A *guru* is a teacher of truth. As we have seen, your baggage is your guru, your glasses are your guru, your undergarments are your guru, your clothes are your guru, your closet is your guru, and cleaning is your guru. Everything is your guru. By playfully cleaning out your closet, you will have discovered an avenue to the most profound self-love. You will have had the opportunity to connect with the part of yourself that is unchanging. This is who you are.

There is this funny thing that happens once we come to know our unchanging Self. We forget it. We forget that who we are is unchanging. It is the nature of the human mind to focus on all that is changing. So, forgetting is normal. This is what our minds are designed to do. That is why we need reminders and practices to help us remember.

Your "Hell yes!" outfit and the three words that you chose to describe this outfit can function as touchstones reminiscent of your unchanging Self. Touchstones are memories, objects, or in this case, words, that you can return to as needed to remind you of the true you. Here, you are using these touchstones to help you remember who you are. To remember the moment when you saw yourself emerge in the mirror and your feeling of well-being emerged too.

When you notice yourself getting caught up in everything that is changing, and you feel less than, or not enough, you can remind yourself that this feeling of well-being is available to you anytime. The act of changing your clothes can be a touchstone to remind you that you are unchanging.

This noticing to becomes our practice, our *sadhana*, when we are suffering. We notice our attachments to that which is changing, and we remember that we are unchanging. We can do this daily, with our touchstones, each morning when we wake up and get dressed for the day. We can practice bringing our awareness to our thoughts each week when we unload our laundry baskets and hang our clothes back in our closet. And we can do this seasonally.

Each time we clean out our closet, we are deepening our understanding of our unchanging Self.

Awareness looks good on you!

ACKNOWLEDGMENTS

Writing a book about the unchanging Self is an interesting challenge because it cannot be described in words. Spiritual teachings are often shared as metaphors, and I felt inspired to pull my passions together and attempt to share these spiritual lessons using fashion metaphors. There are a few people who understood this vision and to them I owe my deepest gratitude.

Stephanie Gunning, without you this book would still be a collection of videos in a "Fashion Metaphors" playlist on YouTube. Your excitement and guidance have been instrumental in making this book a reality. And you get full credit for the eight-fold path play on words. Thank you.

To Marion "Mugs" McConnell, I am forever grateful that you were my first yoga teacher. You continue to be a beacon of spiritual guidance and well-being. Thank you for introducing me to Hirdaya.

Heidi Groschler (Hirdaya), thank you for introducing me to my unchanging Self. You have held space for me to return home to myself and simultaneously expand into all there is.

To Guru Jagat, you continue to inspire from beyond the veil. You pushed the boundaries of what fashion and style can be for a spiritual teacher and created an amazing community where I met Kerry and Abigail.

To Kerry Wilde, the Soul Stylist, thank you for the conversations we shared that sparked my understanding of self-validation. You witnessed me on my soul style journey. You have been my mentor and my muse.

Abigail Rebecca, Human Design Visibility Mentor, thank you for coaching me to be seen. You shared with me your "successories," and thanks to you, I no longer dim my light.

Mary Catherine Rolston, you planted a seed in my mind and nurtured it. I am grateful to you as my inspiration and writing companion.

To my parents, Fred and Carolyn Dubray, thank you for continually investing in my relentless search for meaning.

Thank you to all my friends and family who have appreciated me for my fashion sense or sense of style. Being seen by you helped me recognize that fashion too, can be a path to self-realization.

Finally, I am eternally grateful to my husband, Alex, for not only sharing his closet with me, but continually choosing to build our lives together. I appreciate all the time and patience Alex and my children, Finley and Emma, have extended to me as I pursue my passion for writing.

CITATIONS

1. Elizabeth Gilbert. *Eat Pray Love: One Woman's Search for Everything Across Italy, India and Indonesia* (New York: Riverhead Books, 2007), p. 196.
2. Shoukei Matsumota. *A Monk's Guide to a Clean House and Mind* (New York: TarcherPerigee, 2018), p. vii.
3. Beano Jokes Team. "Twenty Mirror Jokes That'll Crack You Up!" Beano.com (October 6, 2023).
4. Matsumota, p. 130.
5. Kris Ashley. *Change Your Mind to Change Your Reality: How Shifting Your Thinking Can Unlock Your Health, Your Relationships, and Your Peace of Mind* (Helping People Press, 2023), p. 50.
6. Daniel Reynolds. "RuPaul: 'You Are an Extension of the Power That Created the Universe,'" *Advocate* (July 3, 2016).
7. Michael Singer. "Living from a Deeper Part of Your Being," YouTube video, posted by "Relax and Release," June 29, 1993.
8. Sara Camposarcone. "My Personal Style Journey," YouTube video, posted by Sara Camposarcone, January 28, 2024.
9. Katherine J. Igoe. "I Figured Out My Three Style Words and It Was a Game-Changer," TheZoeReport.com (February 20, 2024).

RESOURCES

Thank you for spending the time reading this book. It's been an honor to teach you my approach to enlightenment through closet cleaning and seasonal wardrobe styling, and I hope you find it useful. Additional resources and worksheets are available on my website.

KerriScott.com

Please share your self-reflections and your seasonal wardrobe with me via social media. Tag #buddhascloset along with before and after photos in these posts. I would love to communicate.

- FACEBOOK: @authorkerriscott
- INSTAGRAM: @i_am_kerri
- PINTEREST: @kerridubray
- TIKTOK: @kerriscottauthor
- X: @kerrilynndubray
- YOUTUBE: @kerriscott2222

ABOUT THE AUTHOR

Astrophysicist turned metaphysician **KERRI SCOTT** is the founder of the Soul Selves Framework, a mindset tool that brings awareness to the patterns of behavior that keep us from becoming our authentic selves, and of the hemp clothing line Soham Design. As a writer, researcher, grief advocate, and thought leader, Kerri helps spiritual seekers find profound self-love without the need for external validation by guiding their awareness inward.

Awakened by grief, Kerri has lived the pain of losing a loved one to suicide after their diagnosis of bipolar disorder. From her awakening journey emerged the Soul Selves Framework. In 2022, she contributed a chapter to the book *Prosperity Codes: How to Attune to & Attract Wealth, Joy and Abundance* (Exalted Publishing House). *Buddha's Closet* is her first full-length book.

Kerri lives on Vancouver Island in Canada with her husband and their two children. When she is not writing or cleaning, Kerri likes to play dress up with the clothes in her closet.

www.ingramcontent.com/pod-product-compliance
Lightning Source LLC
Chambersburg PA
CBHW052149070526
44585CB00017B/2045